JAMES
BEARD'S
SALADS

JAMES BEARD'S SALADS

EDITED BY JOHN FERRONE

THAMES AND HUDSON
NEW YORK, NEW YORK

James Beard's recipes and text are adapted from previously published material and are used by permission of Reed College and the executors of his will.

Copyright ©1997 by John Ferrone

First published in the United States of America in paperback in 1997 by Thames and Hudson Inc., 500 Fifth Avenue, New York, New York, 10110

Library of Congress Catalog Card Number 97–60241
ISBN 0–500–27969–1

Designed, typeset and produced by Liz Trovato Book Design
Cover illustration by Patricia Pardini

Printed and bound in Mexico

EDITOR'S NOTE

All of the recipes and much of the text in this cookbook series are James Beard's and are gathered from many sources—magazine articles, syndicated columns, cookbooks, cooking lessons—covering thirty years of culinary exploration. The choice of recipes gives a fair sampling of his thinking on a variety of foods and cuisines. Although he is associated primarily with American cookery, Beard was always on the lookout for gastronomic inspiration in other parts of the world. These cookbooks offer dishes from Portland to Paris, from Maryland to Mexico. Many of them are Beard favorites that turned up in his cooking classes and cookbooks through the years, but also included are less familiar dishes that deserve to be better known. Recipes and text have been edited for these special editions.

J.F.

BEARD ON SALADS

Although Americans cannot claim to have invented salads, we have undoubtedly given the world all sorts of new versions. Our forte is the main-course salad, a popular luncheon dish all across the country, which the French would describe as a *salade composée,* one of two types of salad; the other being the *salade simple,* made with raw greens or cooked vegetables, with a vinaigrette sauce, usually served with the entree. The *salade composée* encompasses compositions of all kinds of ingredients—greens, fruits, seafood, poultry, meat, cheese, and what have you. In this category belong the chef's salad, the Caesar salad, and all the chicken, shrimp, and lobster salads and mayonnaise salads so dear to the heart of the American cook.

Our attitude to the service of salads is equally variable. In some parts of the country, notably California, salad appears as a first course. Elsewhere, it is served in the traditional fashion, with the main course; or after it, teamed with cheese and crisp French or Italian bread. In the latter case, it is usually a simple green salad with an oil and vinegar dressing.

The national taste has also spawned all kinds of oddities, including salads that contain marshmallows, whipped cream and maraschino cherries, as well as an array of jellied concoctions. Some of the aspics and jellied salads certainly have a place in our culinary repertoire, but the more fanciful offerings should be banned.

Fortunately, sensible culinary forces were at work, too. At the Palace Court in San Francisco the chef invented Green Goddess dressing, with a tinge of anchovy in it, and a new era of salads was born. Then a restaurateur in Tijuana, Mexico, named Cesar created a crisp green salad tossed with cheese, anchovies, a coddled egg, and croutons. Finally someone came up with a salad of mixed greens topped with a julienne of various meats and poultry and strips of cheese, called "the chef's salad." Along with Eggs Benedict this creation became one of the most ubiquitous luncheon dishes in the country. At its best, it can be superb, but for one good salad there are hundreds of indifferent ones. If chefs could see what goes out under their name!

But what could be better than a plain green salad? Just rush out to the kitchen and toss a mess of varied greens with a vinaigrette sauce, eat it quickly while it is crisp, and enjoy something that is all a salad should be.

JAMES BEARD

CONTENTS

Meat and Poultry Salads

CHICKEN AND MACADAMIA NUT SALAD	13
CHICKEN AND SWEETBREAD SALAD	14
DUCK SALAD WITH OLIVES AND NUTS	16
DUCK AND ORANGE SALAD	17
TONGUE AND SPINACH SALAD	18
GREASED PIG SALAD	19
VEAL AND ORZO SALAD	20
BEEF SALAD PARISIENNE	21
KNACKWURST SALAD	22

Seafood Salads

SHRIMP AND CAULIFLOWER SALAD	25
SCALLOP SALAD	26
CRAB AND CABBAGE SALAD	27
DIET CRAB SALAD	28
SMOKED SALMON AND PASTA SALAD	29
CANNELLINI BEAN AND TUNA SALAD	30
SCANDINAVIAN SALAD	31
CODFISH SALAD	32

Vegetable and Other Salads

BIBB, MUSHROOM, AND VIOLET SALAD	37
VINTNER'S SALAD	38

Caesar Salad   39

Beet and Mushroom Salad   40

Scandinavian Cucumber Salad   41

Cucumber and Yogurt Salad   42

Green Been and Tomato Salad   43

Asparagus and Egg Salad   45

A Favorite Guacamole   46

Orange and Radish Salad   47

Roast Peppers and Anchovies   48

Céleri Rémoulade   49

Cole Slaw   50

Greek Salad   51

Health Salad   52

Chinese Summer Salad   53

Potato Salad, Alexandre Dumas   54

Rice Salad   55

Lentil Salad   56

Gruyère Cheese Salad   57

Dressings

Mayonnaise   61

Food Processor Mayonnaise   62

Blender Mayonnaise   62

Mustard Mayonnaise   62

Thousand Island Dressing   63

Vinaigrette Sauce   63

Meat and Poultry Salads

CHICKEN AND MACADAMIA NUT SALAD

Serves 4 to 6

Chicken salads are the most common of all main-dish salads, but they are not always all that they should be. Their success depends on the quality of the chicken meat. For best results, poach a chicken carefully, let it cool, and then strip off both white and dark meat.

2 cups poached, cooled chicken meat (see page 14)

1 tablespoon finely chopped fresh tarragon or 1 teaspoon dried soaked in 2 tablespoons white wine

1/2 cup mayonnaise

1/2 cup sour cream

Salt and freshly ground black pepper to taste

2/3 cup macadamia nuts

Greens

1/4 cup capers

Combine the chicken and tarragon. If using dried, soak it in the wine for 45 minutes. Blend the mayonnaise with the sour cream, and taste for seasoning. Reserve some of the mixture for a garnish. Toss the rest with the chicken and nuts. Arrange on a bed of salad greens. Top with the reserved dressing and garnish with capers.

CHICKEN AND SWEETBREAD SALAD

Serves 6

The combination of chicken and sweetbreads, a great favorite at the turn of the century, has become more or less a rarity. It is well worth reviving.

4- to 5-pound chicken
Salted water
1 onion stuck with 2 cloves
1 rib of celery
Sprig of parsley
Pair of sweetbreads
1 cup sliced cucumber, peeled
  and seeded
1 tablespoon finely cut fresh
  tarragon
Mayonnaise
Greens

GARNISH:
Capers and chopped hard-cooked egg

Put the chicken in a kettle with salted water to cover, and add the onion, celery and parsley. Bring to a boil, cover, and reduce the heat. Poach gently until the white meat is just cooked through, about 1 to 1½ hours. Remove the chicken from the broth and allow to cool.

Blanch the sweetbreads in boiling water for 5 minutes, then plunge them into ice water to firm. Remove the membrane. Poach in half water and half chicken broth for about 10 minutes more. Drain and allow to cool.

Discard the chicken skin. Cut the chicken meat and sweetbreads into bite-size pieces. Combine with the cucumber, tarragon, and enough mayonnaise to bind. Arrange on a bed of crisp greens, and spoon more mayonnaise on top. Garnish with capers and hard-cooked egg.

DUCK SALAD WITH OLIVES AND NUTS

The flavor and texture of cold duck make for one of the best of all salads.

3 cups skinned and cubed roast
    duck meat
1 cup thinly sliced green olives
⅔ cup toasted salted walnuts
    or pecans
1 cup mayonnaise (approx.)
Romaine or Bibb lettuce

GARNISH:
Hard-cooked eggs and pimiento

In a salad bowl, combine the duck meat with the olives and nuts. Toss the mixture with enough mayonnaise to bind and still give it body. Spoon into a bowl or on a platter lined with romaine or Bibb lettuce leaves. Top with additional mayonnaise and garnish with slices of hard-cooked eggs and a few strips of pimiento.

DUCK AND ORANGE SALAD

The flavors of duck and orange have had a long association, and they are combined here in a salad substantial enough for a luncheon dish.

2 cups diced cold, cooked duck

1 large or 2 medium seedless oranges, peeled and cut into sections

1 large red Italian onion, thinly sliced and separated into rings

1 cup raw celery root, cut in fine julienne

Romaine or other lettuce

Mayonnaise flavored with extra lemon juice

Toss the duck, orange sections, onion rings and celery root together. Break up the romaine into a bowl, and top with the duck mixture. Pass the mayonnaise separately.

TONGUE AND SPINACH SALAD

Horseradish gives this salad a bit of a nip. If you are using prepared horse-radish, stir it into the vinaigrette sauce.

1½ cups beef tongue, cut into
   julienne
2½ cups well cleaned, crisp
   spinach leaves
½ cup crisp bacon bits
⅓ cup shredded fresh horseradish
   or 2 tablespoons prepared
   horseradish
½ cup vinaigrette sauce (approx.)

Combine the tongue, spinach, bacon and fresh horseradish in a bowl. Pour in just enough vinaigrette sauce to moisten. Toss well.

GREASED PIG SALAD

This is really a B.L.T. sandwich without the benefit of bread. It was discovered at a small soul food restaurant in Montmartre run by Americans and had become a popular hors d'oeuvre with the French.

Crisp leaves of Boston, romaine or
   Bibb lettuce
Slices of really ripe tomatoes
A slice of red onion (optional)
3 or 4 slices of crisp bacon
Mayonnaise

Arrange a few crisp leaves of lettuce on a plate. Top with tomato slices and maybe a slice of red onion. At the last minute add the bacon. Serve with mayonnaise.

VEAL AND ORZO SALAD

Serves 6

Orzo makes a good stand-in for rice, whether it is served hot or cold, as in this versatile dish, which can be made with beef tongue, ham, chicken, or turkey instead of veal.

1 1/2 cups orzo, cooked and drained
2 cups cooked veal, diced
1 cup finely sliced green onions
1 cup thinly sliced celery or fennel
1/4 cup finely chopped parsley
3/4 cup mayonnaise
1/4 cup yogurt
1/4 teaspoon Tabasco
1/2 teaspoon freshly ground black
    pepper

Allow the orzo to cool slightly, then toss well with the rest of the ingredients. Let stand for 2 hours to cool thoroughly and blend the flavors. Toss again before serving.

BEEF SALAD PARISIENNE

Serves 6

A substantial salad that is best assembled when you have the bounty of leftover beef.

2 pounds lean cold boiled or
    pot-roasted beef
6 potatoes, boiled and sliced
½ pound cooked green beans
1 cucumber, peeled and sliced
4 tomatoes, peeled and cut into sixths
2 cups coarsely chopped celery
1 green pepper, cut into thin strips
⅔ cup vinaigrette sauce
1 tablespoon chopped fresh tarragon
    or 1 teaspoon dried tarragon
2 tablespoons chopped parsley
Greens

GARNISH:
6 hard-cooked eggs, halved; 1 red
onion, sliced; 12 cornichons

Slice the beef and then cut into bite-size squares or strips. Combine with the vegetables. Mix the vinaigrette sauce with the tarragon and parsley, pour over the salad, and toss. Arrange on salad greens in a bowl or deep platter. Garnish with the eggs, onion slices and cornichons.

KNACKWURST SALAD

A salad with German origins and a gutsy change from other meat salads.
Serve it with thin buttered pumpernickel.

6 knackwurst
1 medium onion, finely chopped
6 sour pickles or sweet gherkins,
    thinly sliced
1½ tablespoons Dijon mustard
1 cup mayonnaise
3 tablespoons sour cream
Romaine or other lettuce
Chopped gherkins
Chopped parsley

Poach the knackwurst in water to cover for 15 minutes. When cool, skin them and slice rather thin. Combine with the onion, sliced pickles, mustard, and mayonnaise. Toss well, add the sour cream, and toss again. Arrange on a bed of romaine. Garnish with chopped gherkins and chopped parsley.

SEAFOOD
SALADS

SHRIMP AND CAULIFLOWER SALAD

This salad can also be made with chunks of lobster meat.

1 head raw cauliflower

Vinaigrette sauce

1½ to 2 cups cooked and peeled
    shrimp

Mustard mayonnaise or Thousand
    Island Dressing

Watercress

2 hard-cooked eggs, quartered

Black pitted olives

Break the cauliflower into pieces, wash thoroughly, and cut into paper-thin slices. Marinate in vinaigrette sauce for 2 hours, then drain. Combine with the shrimp, add the mayonnaise or Thousand Island Dressing, and toss. Serve on a bed of watercress, garnished with the quartered eggs and black olives.

SCALLOP SALAD

The scallops are cooked for this salad, but they are also used uncooked in the Spanish dish called Seviche, given under the Variation.

FOR EACH SERVING:

1 cup bay scallops, cooked
1½ cups greens
¼ cup onion rings
2 tablespoons chopped green chilies
¼ cup diced avocado
Vinaigrette sauce

The scallops should be lightly poached in salted water for only a minute or so. Arrange the greens on a dish or in a bowl. Add the scallops, onion rings, chilies, and avocado. Dress with vinaigrette sauce.

VARIATION:

Instead of poaching the scallops, marinate them in lime juice to cover for 1 hour. The lime juice will do the cooking. Drain. Proceed with the recipe.

CRAB AND CABBAGE SALAD

An elegant cousin to cole slaw that makes a piquant first course or main luncheon dish.

1 pound crabmeat

1½ cups finely chopped cabbage

½ cup finely sliced green onion

½ cup canned green chilies, chopped

½ cup finely chopped green or
    red bell peppers

Greens

DRESSING:

6 tablespoons olive oil or salad oil

3 tablespoons vinegar

1 tablespoon sugar

1 teaspoon salt

1 teaspoon mustard seed

½ teaspoon freshly ground
    black pepper

Combine the crabmeat and vegetables in a bowl. Prepare the dressing, which should have a sweet-sour taste. Pour over the salad, and toss gently. Refrigerate for at least an hour before serving. Toss again and serve on a bed of greens.

DIET CRAB SALAD

Serves 4

When mayonnaise and salt are out of bounds, here is an inventive treatment of crab that is safe but flavorful.

1 pound fresh or frozen (thawed and drained) crabmeat
1 cup shredded young carrots
¼ cup minced parsley
2 tablespoons white wine vinegar
1 teaspoon freshly ground black pepper
1 teaspoon grated lemon peel
3 large garlic cloves, crushed
⅓ cup or more plain yogurt
Salad greens

Combine all ingredients, except the greens, in a large bowl, cover, and chill at least 2 hours to mellow the flavors. Remove the garlic cloves. Arrange on salad greens on individual plates.

SMOKED SALMON AND PASTA SALAD

Salmon, fresh or smoked, hot or cold, seems to go well with pasta, and the combination is especially satisfying in this uncomplicated recipe.

1/4 pound smoked salmon

1/4 cup mayonnaise

1/4 cup yogurt

3 tablespoons finely chopped shallots

1 tablespoon finely chopped dill

1/2 pound small pasta—shells,
    bow ties or spirals—cooked
    and drained

Salt and pepper to taste

Cut the salmon into strips about 1/4 inch wide and 1 to 1 1/2 inches long. Blend the mayonnaise, yogurt, shallots and dill together. Add the salmon slivers, and mix well, then toss with the pasta. Taste for seasoning. Chill for at least 2 hours to mellow the flavors.

CANNELLINI BEAN AND TUNA SALAD

Serves 4 to 6

Beans are truly an all-season food, as delicious cold as hot. In this satisfying main dish salad, the smooth, mealy texture of the beans nicely complements the crisp onion and flaky tuna.

6 cups canned cannellini beans,
    well drained, or cooked pea beans
6 tablespoons olive oil
1½ to 2 tablespoons wine vinegar
½ to 1 teaspoon salt
½ teaspoon freshly ground black
    pepper
½ teaspoon dried basil or
    2 teaspoons chopped fresh basil
1 cup finely chopped onion
2 7-ounce cans white meat tuna,
    flaked (preferably packed in
    olive oil)
Chopped fresh basil or parsley
Additional oil and vinegar

Lightly toss the drained beans with a vinaigrette sauce, made with the oil, vinegar, salt and pepper, and basil. Arrange in a serving dish and top with the chopped onion and flaked tuna. Sprinkle with chopped basil and parsley. Pour about 3 tablespoons oil and 2 teaspoons vinegar over the tuna and onions just before serving.

SCANDINAVIAN SALAD

A hearty buffet or main dish salad, beautiful to look at and delicious to eat, and the longer it marinates the better it gets.

12-ounce jar herring tidbits
1 to 1½ cups diced cold tongue
    or veal
1 crisp apple, unpeeled and diced
1 cup diced cooked potatoes
1 cup diced or julienne cooked beets
Mayonnaise
Sour cream (optional)
Greens
Chopped fresh dill or parsley

GARNISH:
Tiny whole cooked beets

Cut the herring in thin pieces and combine with the meat, apples, and vegetables. Toss well with enough mayonnaise to bind or a combination of mayonnaise and sour cream. Pack into a mold. Chill. When ready to serve, unmold on a bed of greens, sprinkle with dill or parsley, and garnish with the tiny beets.

CODFISH SALAD

Serves 6

A barman aboard the S.S. *Independence* used to prepare luncheon dishes for favored passengers. He was from Trieste, and this codfish salad was one of his specialties.

2 pounds filleted salt codfish
6 medium waxy potatoes
3 or 4 red Italian onions
½ cup chopped parsley
1 cup olive oil
¼ cup wine vinegar
1 teaspoon freshly ground black
*   pepper*

GARNISH:
Capers and black olives

Soak the codfish in cold water for 12 hours, changing the water once. Drain and put the fish in a kettle of fresh water. Bring to a boil, reduce the heat, and poach until the fish is just tender. Drain it, let it cool, then flake it.

Boil the potatoes in their jackets until they are just tender, about 20 minutes. Peel them and slice thin. Also peel and very thinly slice the onions.

In a large pottery or glass bowl alternate layers of the flaked fish, sliced potatoes, and sliced onions, with a sprinkling of parsley between each layer. (Reserve some for the top.) Prepare a vinaigrette, mixing the oil, vinegar, and pepper. The codfish will probably supply enough salt. Spoon the dressing over the salad and shake the bowl gently to distribute it, or toss very carefully. Garnish with capers, a few black olives, and the remaining chopped parsley.

VEGETABLE
AND OTHER
SALADS

BIBB, MUSHROOM, AND VIOLET SALAD

Serves 4 to 6

Bibb and mushrooms make a perfectly good combination by themselves, but they turn into an eye-opening salad for company with the addition of fresh violets.

4 to 6 heads Bibb lettuce, cut in quarters
½ pound white mushroom caps, cleaned and thinly sliced
1½ cups fresh violets, stemmed
Vinaigrette sauce made with lemon juice and flavored with basil
2 tablespoons chopped parsley

Bibb lettuce can be very gritty, and since it is being used in quarters, it will require extra care in washing. Dry thoroughly and place in a bowl with the mushrooms and violets. Pour in the vinaigrette and toss. Sprinkle with chopped parsley.

VINTNER'S SALAD

Red wine is in the dressing of this refreshing salad, which makes it a good choice to follow a robust main course, when you've been drinking red wine and want to continue.

3 heads Bibb lettuce

½ head romaine

½ bunch watercress

½ cup walnut halves

½ cup shredded Gruyère cheese

½ cup walnut or olive oil

2 tablespoons red wine

1 tablespoon red wine vinegar

1 teaspoon salt

½ teaspoon freshly ground black pepper

Wash and dry the greens. Tear into small pieces. Place in a salad bowl with the watercress, walnut halves, and cheese. Mix the rest of the ingredients for the dressing. Just before serving, pour over the salad and toss.

CAESAR SALAD

When correctly prepared, this is one of the most delicious salads of all. It should be mixed at the last moment and never allowed to stand.

10 tablespoons olive oil

4 tablespoons butter

4 slices white bread, trimmed and cut into small cubes

3 cloves garlic, peeled and crushed

1 egg, coddled for a minute

1 whole garlic clove, peeled

2 heads crisp romaine leaves, washed and dried

18 to 24 anchovy fillets, cut in pieces

2 tablespoons lemon juice

Freshly ground black pepper

Salt to taste

½ cup freshly grated Parmesan cheese

Heat 2 tablespoons of the oil and the butter in a skillet. Add the bread cubes and crushed garlic, and sauté over moderate heat until the bread is crisp and brown, tossing frequently. Remove the garlic, and transfer the bread cubes to paper toweling to drain.

To coddle the egg, lower gently into a pan of boiling water to cover. Remove from the heat at once, cover, and let stand for just 1 minute.

Rub a salad bowl with the whole garlic clove. Break the romaine leaves into manageable pieces and add to the bowl. Add the rest of the oil, and toss. Then add the anchovies, lemon juice, croutons and a few grinds of pepper. Toss again. Taste a bit of romaine for salt; the anchovies should provide enough. Just before ready to serve, break the egg into the salad, and add the cheese. Toss a final time and eat at once.

BEET AND MUSHROOM SALAD

Serves 4

This unusually good mixed salad goes well with hot or cold lamb, pork or veal.

½ pound firm white mushrooms, wiped clean

3 tablespoons olive oil

½ teaspoon salt

1 teaspoon fresh tarragon, chopped, or ½ teaspoon dried

2 teaspoons wine vinegar

¾ cup fresh cooked or canned beets, sliced

2 tablespoons onion, finely chopped

½ cup orange juice (about half an orange)

Mixed greens of your choice, broken, about 5 to 6 cups

Additional oil and vinegar or lemon juice, if needed

2 tablespoons chopped parsley

Slice the mushrooms into a bowl, and add the oil, salt, tarragon and vinegar. Gently toss, then cover and let stand for an hour. In another bowl mix the beets, chopped onion, and orange juice, and also let stand for an hour. Place the broken lettuce leaves in a salad bowl, add the mushrooms and beets, with their dressings, and toss well. Add oil and vinegar or lemon juice to taste, if needed. Sprinkle with chopped parsley.

SCANDINAVIAN CUCUMBER SALAD

Serves 4

The cucumber is about as universal a vegetable as there is, and is found in salads around the world. The Scandinavians use it as we do cole slaw, as the accompaniment to many different dishes.

2 medium-sized cucumbers or 1 long
    Chinese or English cucumber
½ cup cider or white-wine vinegar
2 tablespoons water
½ teaspoon salt
3 tablespoons sugar
⅛ teaspoon freshly ground black
    pepper
3 to 4 tablespoons finely chopped
    fresh dill or half dill, half
    parsley

If they are big, waxy, coarse cucumbers, peel them, split in two, and scrape out the seeds. Leave the Chinese or English cucumber unpeeled. In either case slice very thin, salt lightly and put in a colander. Allow to drain for an hour or so, then rinse briefly under cold water and pat dry. Make a sweet-sour dressing with the rest of the ingredients. Pour the dressing over the cucumbers, cover with plastic wrap, and let stand for at least 3 hours before serving, by which time the cucumbers will have wilted.

CUCUMBER AND YOGURT SALAD

Serves 4

This combination is typically Syrian or Turkish.

2 large cucumbers
2 teaspoons salt
1 cup yogurt
*1/4 teaspoon freshly ground black
  pepper*
1 tablespoon lemon juice
1 tablespoon chopped fresh mint
1 tablespoon chopped parsley

Peel the cucumbers, split in half, and scoop out the seeds. Cut in very thin slices or long shreds. Put in a colander, sprinkle with the salt, and let drain for 1 or 2 hours. Then rinse briefly under cold water, drain again, and pat dry.

Mix the yogurt with the pepper and lemon juice. Combine with the cucumbers, mint and parsley. Marinate several hours before serving.

GREEN BEAN AND TOMATO SALAD

Serves 4

1 pound green beans
2 tablespoons finely chopped
    green onion
1½ tablespoons crumbled blue cheese
Lettuce leaves
2 or 3 ripe tomatoes, thinly sliced

DRESSING:
1 small clove garlic, peeled and
    cut in half
¼ teaspoon salt or to taste
½ teaspoon sugar
⅛ teaspoon dry mustard
⅛ teaspoon paprika
⅛ teaspoon whole oregano
Pinch of thyme
Pinch of savory
½ teaspoon grated onion
1 tablespoon lemon juice
2 tablespoons red wine vinegar
¼ cup olive oil

GARNISH:
2 hard-cooked eggs, peeled and sliced
2-ounce jar sliced pimientos, drained
12 ripe olives

Prepare the dressing at least an hour or two before using. Put all the ingredients, except the oil, in a screw-topped jar, and shake to dissolve the salt, sugar and mustard. Add the oil and shake again. Remove the garlic. Shake just before using.

Trim the beans and cut in 1-inch pieces. Drop into a pot of rapidly boiling salted water. Boil, uncovered, until just tender to the bite, about 5 to 7 minutes from the time the water returns to a full boil. Drain and run cold water over the beans, then dry thoroughly. Toss with the green onion, cheese, and dressing. Cover and refrigerate 3 to 4 hours.

To serve, line salad plates with lettuce leaves. Top with a circle of overlapping tomato slices. Spoon the bean salad in a mound on the tomatoes. Garnish with egg slices, pimiento strips and ripe olives.

ASPARAGUS
AND EGG SALAD

Serves 4

A dressed-up version of the traditional asparagus vinaigrette, and a perfect salad for spring, when asparagus is at its best and most abundant.

24 fat spears of asparagus
Greens
4 hard-cooked eggs, quartered
1/2 cup finely cut chives
1/2 cup chopped parsley
Vinaigrette sauce
1/2 cup grated Parmesan cheese

Trim the asparagus so you have the tips and about 3 inches of the stalks. Boil in salted water to cover until just barely tender. (This is best done in an open skillet.) Drain and allow to cool. Arrange on beds of greens like the spokes of a wheel with egg quarters in between. Spoon vinaigrette sauce over all. Sprinkle with chives and parsley, and finally with cheese.

A FAVORITE
GUACAMOLE

Serves 4 to 6

Traditionally served as a dip or sauce, guacamole is equally delicious as a first course salad, on a bed of greens. Of all the innumerable versions, this utterly simple recipe was the Beard kitchen favorite.

2 large ripe avocados
1 or 2 canned green chilies,
  chopped, or 1 finely chopped
  canned jalapeño or serrano chili
2 tablespoons lime juice
1 to 1¼ teaspoons salt
Greens

The avocados should be soft enough to mash but not overripe and spotted. If you are using the small dark-skinned variety, you may need four. Remove the seeds from the green chilies unless you want a zesty flavor. The jalapeño or serrano chili will really make a spicy-hot guacamole.

Skin the avocados, mash them with a fork, and stir in the chilies, lime juice and salt. That's it. If you are not serving the guacamole immediately, cover it tightly with plastic or it will darken. Placing the pit in the center of the mixture also seems to help. When ready to serve, arrange greens on individual plates and add a small mound of guacamole.

ORANGE AND RADISH SALAD

Serves 4

A colorful Moroccan salad called Shlada Dyal Fejjel ou Lichine.

⅓ cup lemon juice
2 tablespoons sugar
¼ teaspoon salt
4 large navel oranges
1 bunch red radishes

Put the lemon juice in a bowl and stir in the sugar and salt until completely dissolved. Using a sharp knife, cut off the peel and pith of the oranges, then slice into neat sections. Wash the radishes, trim off the tops, and coarsely grate. Combine the oranges and radishes in a salad bowl, pour the lemon mixture over them, and toss gently. Refrigerate until chilled.

ROAST PEPPERS AND ANCHOVIES

Serves 12

Green, red or yellow bell peppers are much more flavorful when they have been grilled or broiled until the skin can be scraped off, a process in which the flesh becomes slightly cooked. The Italians like to combine them with anchovies in this classic dish.

12 to 15 red or green bell peppers
8 tablespoons olive oil
1 to 2 tablespoons wine vinegar
1 teaspoon salt
Few grinds of black pepper
2 cans anchovy fillets, drained
2 tablespoons chopped parsley

First "roast" the peppers—on a charcoal grill, under the broiler or over a gas flame—until the skin is well blackened. Cool slightly, then carefully scrape off the skin without tearing the flesh. It should come off easily. Remove the stem and seeds. Cut in quarters or halves. Dress with the olive oil, vinegar, salt and pepper. Let marinate in the dressing for several hours. Remove to a serving plate and combine with the well-drained anchovy fillets and chopped parsley. Serve as a salad or hors d'oeuvre.

VARIATION:

Add a spoonful of capers to the mixture; or capers and tuna fish.

CÉLERI RÉMOULADE

Serves 4

The main ingredient here is celery root or celeriac, a root vegetable that requires a good deal of trimming and peeling. Some recipes call for it to be blanched in boiling water for a minute or so before being cut into julienne. This one uses it raw.

1 pound celery root, peeled and cut
    into matchstick-size julienne
1 cup mayonnaise
2 tablespoons Dijon mustard or
    to taste
Salt
Greens

The celery root is most easily cut into appropriate strips by using the finer julienne disc of a food processor. It can also be done by hand, but it is a laborious process. Put the raw strips in a bowl. Blend the mayonnaise and mustard together; the dressing should have a definite spicy tang. Toss with the celery root. Taste for salt. Let stand for an hour. Serve on greens as a first course.

COLE SLAW

Serves 4 to 6

The quintessential American vegetable salad. This version approximates the sweet-sour effect of a boiled dressing with much less work.

2-pound head of cabbage, finely
  shredded
Salted water
1 cup mayonnaise
½ cup sour cream
Juice of 1 lemon
1 tablespoon sugar
1 teaspoon dry mustard
Salt and freshly ground black
  pepper to taste

Put the cabbage in a bowl, cover with cold salted water, and let soak for an hour. Drain. Mix the other ingredients, and blend with the cabbage. Let mellow for an hour or so before serving.

VARIATION:

Mix 1 tablespoon of horseradish into the dressing.

GREEK SALAD

Serves 6

The familiar salad served in Greek restaurants has no fixed formula and varies a good deal in content. This one comes from the proprietor of New York's former Coach House restaurant.

2 garlic cloves, split

1 teaspoon salt

2 heads Boston lettuce, shredded

1 head romaine lettuce, shredded

6 radishes, sliced

1 bunch green onions, sliced

1 medium cucumber, peeled and
   sliced

1 green pepper, cut into thin rings

3 ripe tomatoes, cut in wedges

12 Greek olives

1 cup crumbled feta cheese

8 anchovy fillets

¼ cup light olive oil

Juice of 2 lemons

Freshly ground black pepper

½ teaspoon oregano

1 tablespoon chopped Italian
   parsley

Rub a large salad bowl with the garlic cloves and salt. Discard the garlic. Add the lettuce, vegetables, olives, cheese, and anchovies. Beat the olive oil with the lemon juice, and pour over the salad. Sprinkle with pepper to taste, the oregano and parsley, and toss.

HEALTH SALAD

This delicious and attractive combination isn't really a health salad, but it is often called that when served in health food shops. It can be extended with the addition of 1 cup of raw young peas, shredded snow peas or sliced raw mushrooms.

Chicory, Bibb or other lettuce
2 cups freshly shredded raw carrots
2 cups freshly shredded young
*   raw beets*
1 cup or more freshly shredded
*   Japanese radish or black radish*
1½ cups freshly shredded raw
*   young turnips*
2 small cucumbers, seeded and
*   shredded*
Cherry tomatoes
Celery, cut into thin sticks
Vinaigrette sauce (½ to ¾ cup)

Arrange the lettuce on a platter. Mound the vegetables in separate piles on the greens, with an eye for color. Garnish with cherry tomatoes and celery. Let eaters help themselves. Pass the vinaigrette sauce separately.

CHINESE SUMMER SALAD

Certain flowers are edible and make an intriguing addition to salads. This one uses nasturtium leaves and flowers. It is delicious with cold chicken or cold teriyaki steak slices.

1 pint bean sprouts, washed and picked over

4 tablespoons sesame oil

2 tablespoons dry sherry

6 tablespoons olive oil

2 tablespoons soy sauce

2 tablespoons lemon juice

Freshly ground black pepper to taste

2 cups shredded Chinese cabbage

1 head Boston lettuce leaves, washed and dried

12-ounce can bamboo shoots, cut into long spears

12 to 14 nasturtium leaves, washed and cut into strips

3 or 4 nasturtium flowers

Toss the bean sprouts with a mixture of the sesame oil and sherry. Combine the olive oil, soy sauce, lemon juice, and pepper. Pour half of it over the cabbage and toss. Arrange the lettuce on a platter or in a shallow bowl. Mound the bean sprouts on one half of the platter and the cabbage on the other. Make a border of the bamboo shoots. Garnish with the nasturtium leaves and flowers. Spoon the remaining olive oil dressing over the bamboo shoots. Serve with additional dressing if needed.

POTATO SALAD, ALEXANDRE DUMAS

Serves 6

A French-style potato salad dressed with wine and oil instead of the more usual mayonnaise.

6 largish new potatoes in their skins
Salt and freshly ground black pepper
1/2 cup olive oil
1/2 cup dry white wine
1 tablespoon white wine vinegar
1/2 cup chopped parsley
1/2 cup chopped chives or green onions

Boil the potatoes in salted water until just tender, about 20 minutes. Drain and cool slightly, then peel. Cut into slices and put into a bowl. Sprinkle with salt and pepper to taste.

While they are still warm, pour the oil and wine over them. Allow to marinate until cooled. Add the rest of the ingredients, and toss carefully.

RICE SALAD

The success of a rice salad depends on achieving fluffy, well-drained rice, with each kernel separate—rice that can hold. This is the secret: When rice has reached the tenderness you like, drain it, add a couple of table-spoons of oil, and toss it well with two forks—not spoons.

1 cup raw rice
2 or 3 tablespoons oil
1 cup green onions or red Italian
*   onion, finely chopped*
1 cup peeled, seeded and finely
*   diced cucumber*
½ cup finely diced green or
*   red pepper*
1 cup peeled, seeded, and chopped
*   tomato*
Chopped fresh basil and parsley
*   to taste*
Vinaigrette sauce
Greens

GARNISH:
Rings of pepper, strips of green
onion, thin slices of tomato

Cook the rice according to your favorite method. Drain, if need-ed, add the oil, and toss with two forks to coat each grain of rice. Add the vegetables, chopped herb, and vinaigrette sauce, made with 5 parts olive oil to 1 part lemon juice or wine vinegar, and salt and freshly ground black pepper. Allow to cool thoroughly but do not chill. Arrange on a bed of greens, and garnish with the pepper, onion, and tomato.

This is superb with foods from the outdoor grill—steaks, chops, chicken, or butterflied leg of lamb.

LENTIL SALAD

Ideal for a picnic or buffet party because it travels well and holds up for days. It is excellent with cold meats, such as ham, boiled beef, or chicken.

2 cups lentils
2 teaspoons salt
1 onion stuck with 2 cloves
1 bay leaf
1 teaspoon thyme
1/2 cup olive oil
1 1/2 cups finely sliced green onions
1/4 cup finely chopped pepper
1 garlic clove, finely chopped
3 to 4 tablespoons wine vinegar
1 1/2 teaspoons freshly ground
*   black pepper*
1/2 cup chopped parsley

Put the lentils in a pot with water to more than cover. Add the salt, onion, bay leaf and thyme. Bring to a boil, reduce the heat, and cover. Simmer until the lentils are just tender but still firm, about half an hour. Drain well, and toss gently with 3 tablespoons of the oil. Let cool slightly, then add the rest of the ingredients, except the parsley. Toss again. Taste for seasoning. Allow to mellow in the refrigerator for at least several hours. Just before serving, add the parsley, and toss once more.

GRUYÈRE CHEESE SALAD

The Swiss, who produce some of the finest cheeses, have a gift for finding ways to use them in almost every part of a meal, including the salad course. This particular salad was discovered in a favorite brasserie in Lausanne.

2 pounds Switzerland Gruyère
    cheese, finely shredded
2 cups sliced green onions
1 cup sliced stuffed green olives
1 cup olive oil
¼ cup wine vinegar
1 heaping tablespoon Dijon mustard
1 teaspoon salt
¼ teaspoon freshly ground
    black pepper
Greens

GARNISH:
Additional green onions and
    green olives

In a bowl combine the grated cheese, green onions and olives. Prepare a vinaigrette sauce, mixing together the olive oil, vinegar, mustard, and salt and pepper. Toss the cheese mixture with the dressing, and let it stand for half an hour. Then arrange in a salad bowl lined with crisp greens. Garnish with sliced green onions and olives.

DRESSINGS

MAYONNAISE

Makes 1 ¾ cups.

Both the eggs and oil should be at room temperature to help prevent curdling. Homemade mayonnaise will keep a week under refrigeration.

2 egg yolks
1½ cups oil (half olive, half
  peanut)
1 tablespoon vinegar or lemon juice
1 teaspoon salt
½ teaspoon dry or Dijon mustard

Mayonnaise can be mixed by hand with a fork, whisk or egg beater; or with an electric mixer, blender or food processor. If using a fork, prepare in a soup plate; if using a whisk, egg beater or electric mixer, prepare in a bowl. (See separate recipes for the blender or food processor.) First beat the yolks together with the salt and mustard. Then beat in the oil slowly, one teaspoon at a time, till the emulsion begins to thicken. Gradually increase the amount of oil. When the mixture becomes very thick, beat in the vinegar. Taste for seasoning.

Note: Raw eggs sometimes carry salmonella bacteria, which can cause food poisoning. To avoid any risk, you can use commercial mayonnaise or seek out a recipe that calls for lightly cooking the egg yolks. James Beard would have resorted to neither alternative.

FOOD PROCESSOR MAYONNAISE

Makes 1 3/4 cups

1 whole egg
1 tablespoon vinegar or lemon juice
1 teaspoon salt
1/4 teaspoon pepper
1 1/2 cups oil (half olive, half peanut)

Put the egg, vinegar, and salt and pepper in the processor and pulse 2 or 3 seconds. Then, with the machine running, slowly—very slowly at first—pour in the oil until the mixture emulsifies.

BLENDER MAYONNAISE

Makes 1 1/4 cups

1 whole egg
2 teaspoons wine vinegar or lemon juice
1/2 teaspoon salt
1 teaspoon dry or Dijon mustard
1 cup oil (half olive, half peanut)

Put the egg, vinegar, salt and mustard in the blender container. Turn to high for a few seconds, then start to dribble oil through the top till the mixture emulsifies and thickens, about 1 minute.

MUSTARD MAYONNAISE

To one cup of mayonnaise add 1 tablespoon Dijon mustard or 1 teaspoon dry mustard.

THOUSAND ISLAND DRESSING

To 1 cup mayonnaise add 1 tablespoon of finely chopped onion, 3 tablespoons of chili sauce, 1 chopped hard-cooked egg, and a touch of dry mustard.

VINAIGRETTE SAUCE

Makes 1/2 cup

This is also called "French Dressing." It is best to make it fresh for each salad.

6 tablespoons olive or vegetable oil
2 tablespoons wine vinegar
1/2 to 1 teaspoon salt
1/2 teaspoon freshly ground
*   black pepper*

Blend the ingredients together thoroughly. Adjust the vinegar content and salt and pepper to suit the salad or the individual palate.

VARIATION:

Substitute lemon juice for the vinegar for certain salads.